**HERE'S ELVIS . . .** Newest sensation of rock 'n' roll, Elvis Presley of Memphis, Tenn., guests on Berle Show Tues., 8 p. m., Ch. 4.

**7:30** ❷ — **Name That Tune,** musical quiz, George De Witt.
❹—**Dinah Shore Show.**
❺—**Waterfront,** Drama, Preston Foster.
❼ ⑧ —★— **Warner Brothers** ... "Cheyenne

*for Grelun*

# Shock, Rattle & Roll

## ELVIS PHOTOGRAPHED DURING THE MILTON BERLE SHOW

FROM THE MICHAEL OCHS ARCHIVES

DESIGN **GER RIJFF, ECCO FATTO! / JEANPAUL COMMANDEUR** TEXT **TREVOR CAJIAO**

BLANDFORD

"After Presley was on I received 700,000 pan letters. Not fan mail - *pan* mail. It was all on my shoulders, they put the burden on my shoulders. It was like, 'Uncle Miltie, we'll never watch you again. How dare you put on a young man like that to gyrate and do those motions which are disgusting on a show like yours which is about family entertainment'."

**MILTON BERLE**

# Shock, Rattle & Roll

When talking about classic film footage of the young Elvis Presley, his rendition of 'Hound Dog' from 'The Milton Berle Show' must come top of the list. Featured in many a documentary since (and even used in the recent Oscar-scooping 'Forrest Gump'), it's one of those true gems that always stands up to repeated viewing.

And yet it was the most controversial of all his early (pre-Ed Sullivan) TV appearances. The critics panned it and attacked him for bringing his "suggestive" and "downright obscene" stage act to prime time television. One reporter commented that his routine was "in appalling taste", another described it as "totally vulgar".

Today, of course, we look back on such ridiculous ravings with a wry smile and wonder just how anyone with an ounce of sense could get so hot under the collar about some guy on TV wiggling his legs and moving to music. In these days of end-to-end music videos being pumped out on MTV ad nauseum, each one trying to out-do the other for maximum effect, it's difficult to relate to the controversy Elvis created via his early appearances on American television in the Eisenhower era. They seem tame now, and yet at the time it was as if the world was coming to an end because of the effect this young 'hoodlum' from Memphis was having on the morals of the teenage population with that nasty rock n roll beat of his.

He'd been on national television before and the critics hadn't said too much about him, but his appearance with Milton Berle in June of '56 sent them scurrying to their type-

writers to punch out headlines such as 'Final Berle Show Revoltingly Sexy' and 'Obscene Presley'.

## Uncle Miltie

Milton Berle, a stalwart of American TV in the '50s, was a comedian in the vaudeville tradition. Known as 'Uncle Miltie' and 'The Thief Of Bad Gags', he was from a much earlier generation and yet of all the personalities who presented Elvis as a guest on their shows (Tommy and Jimmy Dorsey, Steve Allen and Ed Sullivan), he appeared to be the most sympathetic and seemed more tuned in to what was going on than the others.

## Tearing up the West Coast

Elvis flew out from Memphis to the West Coast on June 2nd for two shows the next day at the Oakland Auditorium Arena. The local press reported that over 6,400 "madly screaming fans" attended the two performances and witnessed their 21-year-old hero belting it out in what the 'Oakland Tribune' described as "a gyrating, knee-knocking, tear-them-apart style of whipping out a song with a vicious driving beat".

Following the shows, Elvis and his entourage travelled onto L.A., booking in at the Knickerbocker Hotel around 4.30am. After a few hours sleep it was off to the NBC-TV studios in Burbank and rehearsals for 'The Milton Berle Show'.

Gordon Stoker of The Jordanaires remembers Berle being a little uneasy: "Milton was very nervous - far more so than on any other show I'd seen him on. This was his last show of the season and he knew that having Elvis on would kick his ratings way up - I'm sure that's why he was so nervous. He tried to be funny during the rehearsals, saying things that were not funny, especially to Elvis, but Elvis was - as always - very courteous to him and, believe it or not, spent a lot of the rehearsal time trying to make Milton feel comfortable!"

The two had worked together before, back in April when Elvis sang 'Heartbreak Hotel' and 'Blue Suede Shoes' during a remote broadcast of Berle's show from the U.S.S. Hancock in San Diego. At that time Berle had booked Presley only as a favour to his agent, Abe Lastfogel. But things were different now. By the time of his second appearance with Berle, 'Heartbreak Hotel' was just finishing an eight-week stint at No.1 on the 'Billboard' charts, 'Blue Suede Shoes' had made the Top 20 as an EP track, his debut LP ('Elvis Presley') was the best-selling pop album and his latest release, 'I Want You, I Need You, I Love You', was rapidly climbing the charts and would also eventually hit the top spot. His popularity (and notoriety) was spreading fast. Hollywood had shown an interest, his stage shows were drawing sell-out audiences, his controversial "bump-and-grind" stage antics were the talk of the media and rock n roll in general was gaining more of a foothold in the entertainment industry day-by-day. 'Presley-mania' had arrived and the whole world was about to change. The dull pop scene of the early '50s was being shattered by the rock n roll explosion - and Elvis was leading the way.

**"Well they said you was high classed..."**

The final 'Milton Berle Show' of the season was broadcast over NBC from 8.00 to 9.00pm (EST) on June 5th 1956. As well as Elvis, the show featured guest appearances from orchestra leader Les Baxter (performing his No.1 hit 'The Poor People Of Paris'), movie star Debra Paget (who in a couple of months would co-star alongside Elvis in 'Love Me Tender'), TV personality Irish McCalla (of 'Sheena, Queen Of The Jungle' fame), comedian Arnold Stang, and seven-year-old novelty singer / actor Barry Gordon (who later in the year would appear as Tom Ewell's newspaper boy in the classic rock n roll movie 'The Girl Can't Help It').

It was a typical variety show of the day. Berle cracked jokes on topical subjects (Grace Kelly's marriage to Prince Ranier, the Primary Elections, 'Confidential' magazine etc.), joined some of his guests in comedy routines and presented them singing and dancing, all the while giving regular plugs to the show's sponsors, RCA.

Elvis was featured twice. Following the first of the show's commercial breaks, Berle announced "Here he is - the new singing sensation all over the country - Elvis Presley!", and the camera panned centre stage to reveal Tupelo's finest in all his glory. Dressed in an over-size sport coat with black slacks and a two-tone shirt, and clinging to his adjustable microphone stand as if his life depended on it (he'd only ever been on TV without his guitar once before - during one of his 'Stage Show' appearances), here was THE REAL THING!



With his regular trio of Scotty Moore, Bill Black and D.J. Fontana behind him, the kid they would come to call The King cut loose with 'Hound Dog', a song he'd picked up in Las Vegas from lounge act Freddie Bell & The Bellboys. It would be another month before he'd record the song, but he'd been doing it in his stage act and was eager to perform it on TV.

A magnificent performance (and quite different from the eventual record release), its visual presentation was dynamic with Elvis incorporating many of his loose-as-a-goose stage antics and "bump-and-grind" movements into the proceedings. The slowed-down, bluesy ending was a master stroke, adding a playful sleaziness the likes of which TV viewers of 1956 had simply never seen before.

"How about my boy?" asked an obviously well-chuffed Uncle Miltie as the number drew to a close and the duo embarked on a humorous discussion regarding Elvis' popularity. "I don't like it", joked Elvis, "...all these girls screaming, always tearing your clothes off, always, y'know, trying to rip you

apart, always trying to kiss you...I don't like that". "You don't?", enquired Berle. "No", said Elvis, setting up Uncle Miltie's punch-line of "Someone must have stomped on his head with those blue suede shoes...".

Continuing the play-acting, Elvis remarked that personally he'd prefer a more sedate type of girl - someone like Debra Paget. Cue the lady herself in a flowing ball gown who, instead of being the cool, sophisticated type Berle suggested she was ("She's not in your league. Stick to 'Heartbreak Hotel' and stay away from the Waldorf."), turns out to be a fan and grabs Elvis, swooning over him as she kisses him in a passionate embrace. "How do you feel now, man?" asks Berle. "Cool, man" says Elvis.

**"Give me the good old Rudy Vallee days..."**

Later in the show, in a scene set in the 'Colony Music Shop', Elvis joined Berle in a brief skit poking fun at Presleymania. A group of fans are waiting for their hero to arrive for an autograph-signing session. Uncle Miltie assures them that he knows Elvis well, but when Elvis arrives - accompanied by his band and The Jordanaires - he fails to recognise him. "Hey, what are the Ritz Brothers doing here?" asks Berle.

In the ensuing confusion the fans mob Berle instead of Elvis, tearing his jacket to shreds in the process. A dishevelled Uncle Miltie addresses the camera with a deadpan look and the comment, "Give me the good old Rudy Vallee days..." Elvis and his guys then swing into 'I Want You, I Need You, I Love You', the follow-up to 'Heartbreak Hotel' and his next No.1.

After the song, in what looked like a genuine show of affection, Berle announced "I don't think I'm revealing any secrets when I say that Elvis Presley is the fastest rising young singer in the entertainment industry today". He went on to present him with a 'Billboard' Triple Crown Award for 'Heartbreak Hotel', which had topped the sales, juke box and disc jockey listings in both the pop and country categories as well as also denting the rhythm and blues charts.

Berle smiled. Presley smiled. Everyone was happy. Well, *almost* everyone...

**More popular than Sgt. Bilko**

For the first time all season, 'The Milton Berle Show' beat Phil Silvers' ever-popular 'Sgt. Bilko' (over on the rival CBS network) in the ratings. But the press were quick to jump on Elvis' "vulgar" and "animalistic" performance of 'Hound Dog'. 'Variety' declared that his appearance "certainly added no values to the programme"; the 'New York Times' reported "Mr. Presley has no discernible singing ability"; whilst Ben Gross of the 'Daily News' fumed that Elvis, "who rotates his pelvis, was appalling musically. Also he gave an exhibition that was suggestive and vulgar, tinged with the kind of animalism that should be confined to dives and bordellos." He closed his review with "What amazes me is that Berle and NBC-TV should have permitted this affront".

Prompted by the negative press reports, the top brass at NBC announced that for his next scheduled appearance on the network - 'The Steve Allen Show' on July 1st - Elvis would not be allowed to "bump-and-grind". Unfortunately, Elvis - for whatever reason (probably just to keep the peace) - went along with the decision and, dressed in a tuxedo, sang to a basset hound instead in a rather putrid attempt to try and quell all the controversy. It was pathetic. It may well have pleased the smug Steve Allen (a rock n roll hater), but Elvis' ever-growing legions of fans weren't amused. "We want the gyratin' Elvis" they demanded. They got their wish later in the year when he made his first of three appearances on 'The Ed Sullivan Show' on CBS. But that's another story and another book (see Tutti Frutti's '60 Million TV Viewers Can't Be Wrong').



**The Real Elvis**

As the great James Brown once put it: "Elvis taught white America to *get down*!". He did so against much adversity from numerous fools in the media who really believed he was the Devil incarnate let loose to disrupt the morals of the youth and society itself. These days, of course, things are a lot different. Elvis Presley's tremendous contribution and influence on the whole history of popular music is well documented, and that impact came about through several key points in his early career: the legendary Sun recordings, the groundbreaking 'Heartbreak Hotel' and, of course, his eye-opening early TV appearances amongst them. His performance of 'Hound Dog' on the June 5th 1956 edition of 'The Milton Berle Show' stands out as one of the greatest moments of his whole career. Elvis in his prime. **The real Elvis**. One of the truly magical moments of all time.

TREVOR CAJIAO

*(Editor of 'Now Dig This' and 'Elvis - The Man & His Music')*

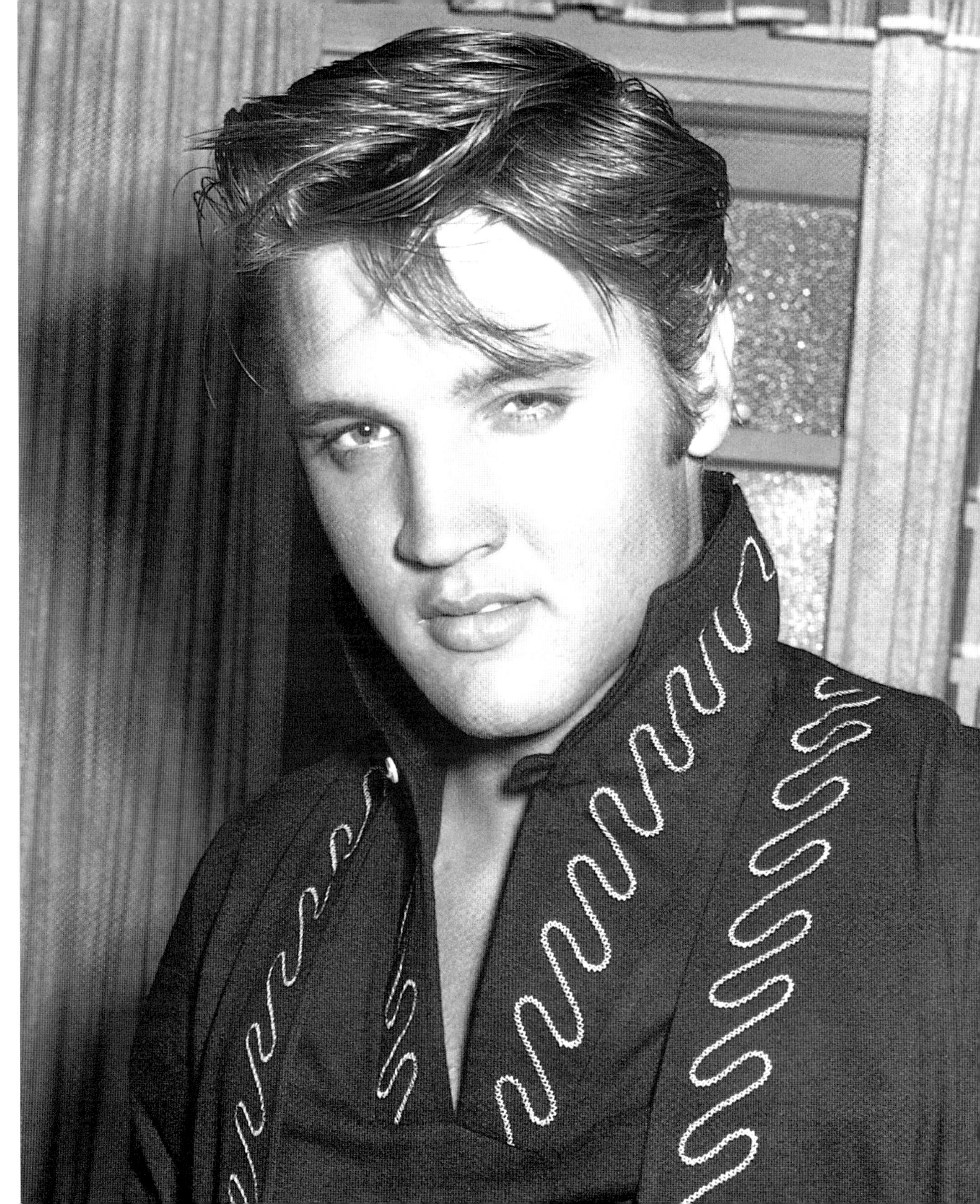

*L.A., June 5, 1956*

*L.A., June 5, 1956*

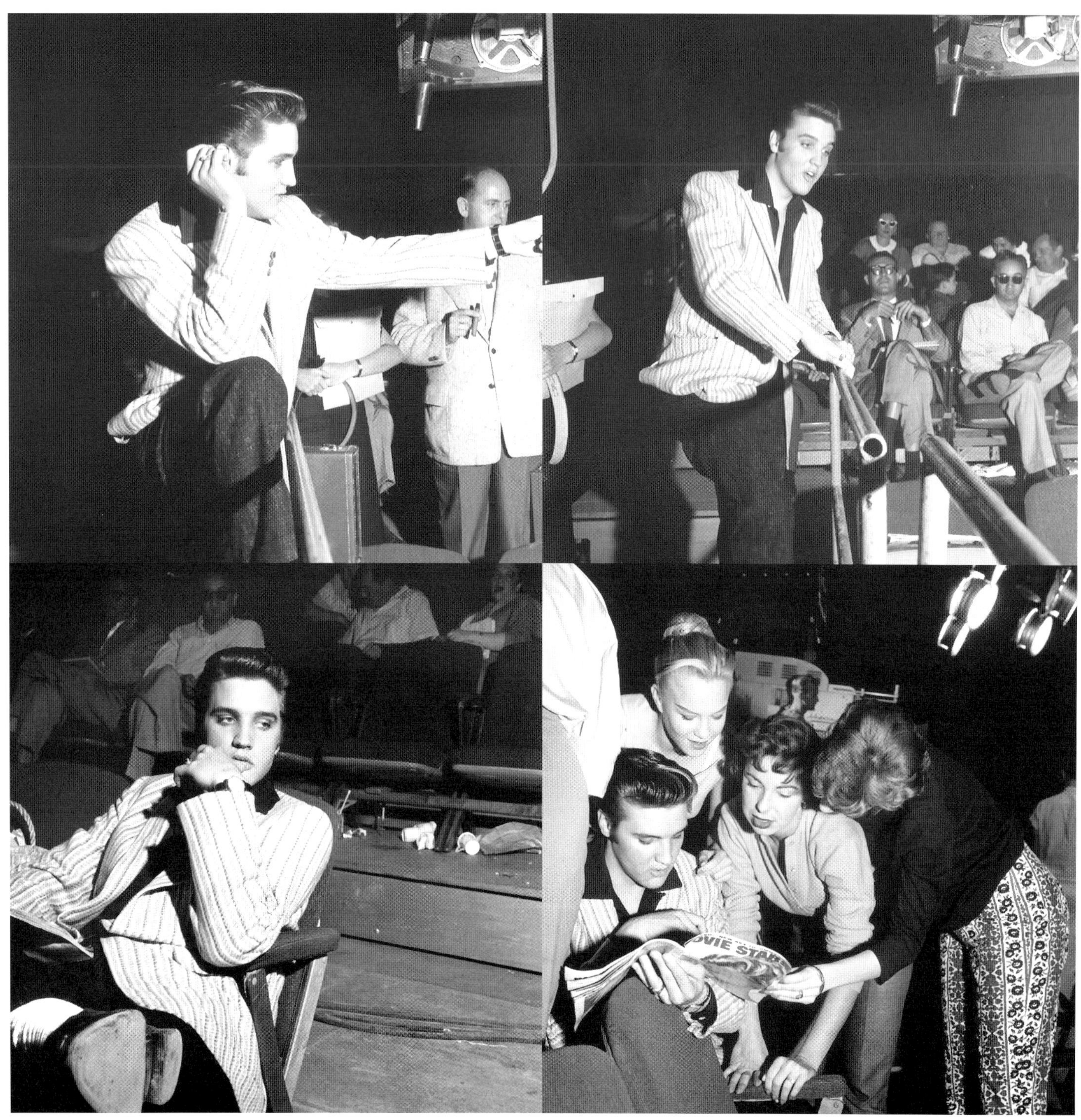
OVIE STAR

*L.A., June 5, 1956*

*L.A., June 5, 1956*

L.A., June 5, 1956

*L.A., June 5, 1956*

L.A., June 5, 1956

*L.A., June 5, 1956*

Gibson

*L.A., June 5, 1956*

*L.A., June 5, 1956*

L.A., June 5, 1956

*L.A., June 5, 1956*

*L.A., June 5, 1956*

*L.A., June 5, 1956*

L.A., June 5, 1956

NBC

*L.A., June 5, 1956*

*L.A., June 5, 1956*

*L.A., June 5, 1956*

68

L.A., June 5, 1956

Gibson

*L.A., June 5, 1956*

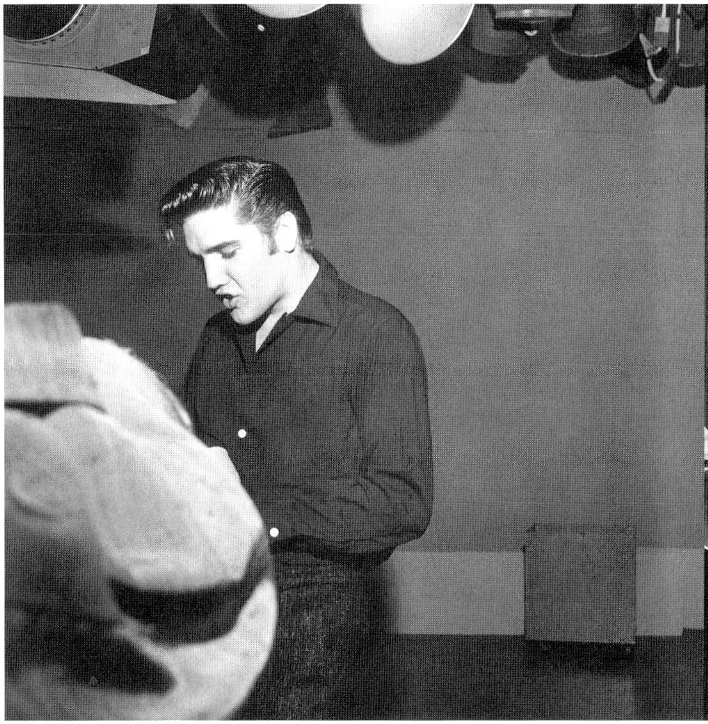

L.A., June 5, 1956

*L.A., June 5, 1956*

COLONY

CENTURY
SIC
MUSIC

## TUESDAY JUNE 5

it's the story of the role played by Maj. Tom Howie in the Normandy campaign. Peter Graves, Nick Dennis. (Film)

CAST

Maj. Tom Howie....................Peter Graves
Sgt. Chiaco..............................Nick Dennis
Lt. Morgan............................Robert Cossen
Maj. Bingham..........................Ed Kemmer
Gen. Gerhardt...................Morris Ankrum
Gen. Cota............................Frank Gerstle

**13 LIFE OF RILEY—Comedy**

Riley and Otto are on the "Waterfront" to repair the wing of a plane. When they discover a coded message in the wing, they find that their interest in the message is violently shared by a pair of gangsters. William Bendix is featured as Riley. With Marjorie Reynolds.

**9:00 2 KIT CARSON—Western**

"Range Masters." Kit is sent to investigate the trial of a man accused of murdering his cattle foreman. (Film)

**4 MILTON BERLE—Comedy**

For his last show of the season, Uncle Miltie has a varied guest lineup. Scheduled to visit tonight are Elvis Presley, the new singing sensation; Debra Paget, who will sing and dance; Arnold Stang as Francis; Irish McCalla, who plays in the *Sheena* series; Les Baxter and orchestra.

**5 13 PHIL SILVERS—Comedy**

Bilko plays Cupid. He's trying to persuade a society girl to be queen to Pvt. Doberman's king in the post motor pool's Mardi Gras fete. Doberman's got a secret crush on the haughty socialite. Maurice Gosfield, Constance Ford. (Film)

**9 DANNY THOMAS—Comedy**

*See 7 P.M. (13) for details.*

**9:30 2 5 13 NAVY LOG—Drama**

"The Plebe." A member of the Annapolis boxing team undergoes an arduous test imposed by the disciplinary rules of the Naval Academy. John Wilder. (Film)

**5 MR. DISTRICT ATTORNEY**

Mr. D.A. finds that a simple manslaughter case is complicated by conflicting testimony of two witnesses. David Brian stars as D. A. Paul Garrett. (Film)

**9 NEWS—Lionel Schwan**

**13 NEWS AND WEATHER**

**10:05 4 TO BE ANNOUNCED**

**10:10 2 WEATHER—John Yates**

**9 SPORTS—Sam Molen**

**10:15 2 DUFFERS' DELITE—Golf**

Guests: pro Bud Elford; the winner of the *Duffer's Delite* Tourney in Albany; and pupils from Hiawatha and Moila.

**9 MOVIE—Drama**

*Tuesday Movie:* "You Only Live Once." An ex-convict is framed by his former cellmate. Henry Fonda, Sylvia Sidney are the featured actors.

**13 SHOW TIME—Drama**

"The Big Jump." A couple, prospecting for uranium on a lonely western plateau, grows suspicious of a young man who has offered help. Nancy Gates, John Bryant, Don Haggerty, James Flavin head tonight's cast. (Film)

**10:30 5 DO YOU TRUST YOUR WIFE**

*See 8:30 P.M. (2) for details.*

**10:35 4 NEWS**

**10:45 2 MOVIE—Drama**

*Sandman Theater:* "Hard Guy." The story of a girl's romance with the son of an ex-governor. Jack LaRue, Mary Healy.

**4 SPORTS AND WEATHER**

**13 FILM FEATURE**

Topic: "Sunny Skyways." (Film)

**11:00 4 Tonight—Steve Allen**

Steve and the gang are having a barbecue on 45th St. Guests include vocalist Johnny Johnston and dancer Chita Rivera.

**5 NEWS**

**13 SPORTS**

**11:05 5 MOVIE—Comedy**

*Studio Five:* "The Gay Desperado." Com-

*L.A., June 5, 1956*

L.A., June 5, 1956

L.A., June 5, 1956

RCA-VICTOR'S

LATEST STAR **ELVIS PRESLEY**

★ You saw him last night on the Milton Berle Show!

★ You can hear him in person at the San Diego Arena Tonight & Tomorrow Night!

**COME IN AND BUY HIS RCA-VICTOR RECORDS NOW— WHILE THEY LAST!**

✓ Heart Break Hotel ✓ Blue Suede Shoes
✓ Tutti Fruitti ✓ I Got A Woman ✓ Many Others

**Buy His RCA Album on 45 RPM or LP and Save!**

IS PRESLEY TELLS OWN STORY:

# Don't Pay No Attention to Critics—
# I'm Just Gonna Go on Bein' Ol' Elvis'

**"DIGGING" ELVIS . . .** Bobby-soxers' delight Elvis Presley, "sends" all about himself to Atra Baer, who is intrigued by his crimson velvet shirt, dazzling rings and hair-do.

A BLANDFORD BOOK

First published in the UK 1997 by Blandford
A Cassell Imprint
Cassell Plc, Wellington House, 125 Strand, London WC2R OBB



Distributed in the United States by Sterling Publishing Co., Inc.,
387 Park Avenue South, New York, NY 10016-8810

A cataloging-in-Publication Data entry for this title is available from the British Library

ISBN 0-7137-2690-3

Design by Ger Rijff, Ecco Fatto!/Jeanpaul Commandeur
Text by Trevor Cajiao

Printed and bound in Singapore by Kyodo Printing Co.

**SOME OF THE NEGATIVES OF THE PHOTOGRAPHES ON PAGES 33 & 34 WERE DAMAGED BEYOND REPAIR**